MW00718589

You Can Have What You Say, If You Stop Saying What You Have!!

To Mrs Nancy Dickens

Thank you for sowing good seed into good H ground

Gregory White

Bishop. Gregg White

Copyright © 2011
You Can Have What You Say, If You Stop Saying What You Have!!!
G. L. White Ministries
www.glwhiteministries.webs.com

Printed in the United States of America

Catalogued in the Library of Congress – Publication Department

ISBN – 978-0-9839248-0-7

Editorial Assistance
Jabez Books Writers' Agency
(A Division of Clark's Consultant Group)
www.clarksconsultantgroup.com

Unless otherwise stated, scriptural quotations are taken from the King James Version of the Bible.

$\mathcal{D}edication$

This book was birthed on my mother's birthday, July 10, 2009, at a book writing seminar. I would like to dedicate this book to my loving mother, the late Mrs. Eloise H. Williams, who raised me to be the man that I am today. Thank you, mom, for not aborting me and allowing me to live. Thank you, Lord.

$\mathscr{Acknowledgments}$

First of all, I would like to thank my Lord and Savior Jesus Christ for allowing me this opportunity to write this best seller book on His behalf.

And to my friend, my lover, my wife, Theresa M. White, I thank you for being there for me. Just know that I love you always.

I would like to thank my children also Jecobii, Greasean, and Shar'ta Re'da for their understanding and love. My sentiments are summed up in my mother's favorite saying, God loves you and so do I!!!

As well, I would like to thank God for my pastor, Bishop Fred A. Caldwell, Sr., who has been my mentor, spiritual father, and counselor for 14 years at Greenwood Acres Full Gospel Baptist Church. I thank

God for leading me to this great church and to have a loving pastor like Bishop Caldwell. Thank you, Bishop, for allowing the Lord to use you to speak into my life.

Next, I would like to thank my church family of Greenwood Acres Full Gospel Baptist Church for their prayers and support. I especially like to thank Sister Jan Whitaker for the Lord leading her to have a book writing seminar.

And lastly, I like to thank Dr. Shirley K. Clark, my consultant, and Clark Consultant Group for the role they played in making this book a reality. Thank you for the many hours that you spent to make this book a bestseller. I will forever be grateful!

Foreword

The Word teaches us that death and life are in the power of the tongue; and they that love it, shall eat the fruit thereof (Proverbs 18:21). Never before have more true words been spoken. We are living in an era, where people are affixed and mesmerized with what they see, to determine what decisions they will make.

While we look not at the things which are seen, but at the things which are not seen: for the things which are seen are temporary; but things which are not seen are eternal (II Corinthians 4:18).

Minister Gregory White is to be commended, as he approaches this mammoth subject of "you can have what you say, if you stop saying what you have!!" In this book, we are admonished to watch our mouths, and to be very careful what comes forth out of them.

Almighty God has bigger and better things for all of His children. He said, "No good thing will he withhold from them that walk uprightly," (Psalm 84:11b). A holy life before God equates into blessings, joy unspeakable and full of glory. We need to stop saying what we have, and begin saying what God says is already ours. We need to learn to call those things that be not, as though they were. We must stop waiting to see before we say, and start saying what God has said is already ours.

Thanks, Minister White for helping us to change our minds about looking at what we can see in the natural before we start believing God for what we cannot see! God's Word says, "Let the weak say that I am strong," (Joel 3:10b). Whether we feel like it or not because we cannot lie by saying what God says. So, let's believe it and receive it, let's name it and claim it, it's already ours.

"Live forever, Man of God," and Thanks!...for writing this book.

Much, Much Love to ya!

Bishop Fred A. Caldwell, Sr.

Pastor/Teacher

Greenwood Acres Full Gospel B.C.

Shreveport, LA

Table of Contents

Chapter One

SPEAK BIG

(What God Said, He Saw)

"In the beginning God created the heaven and the earth. And the earth was without form, and void; and darkness was upon the face of the deep. And the spirit of God moved upon the face of the waters.

And God said, *Let there be light:* ***and there was light***

And God said, *Let there be firmament in the midst of the waters...and God made the firmament, and divided the waters which were under the firmament...*

*And God said, Let the waters under the heaven be gathered together unto one place, and let the dry land appear; **and it was so.***

*And God said, Let the earth bring forth grass, the herb yielding seed, and the fruit tree yielding fruit after his kind...**and it was so.***

*And God said, Let there be light in the firmament of the heaven to divide the day from the night...**and it was so.***

The Word of God reflects the heart and mind of God. It is a testament of hope and endurance. As well, it is a guidepost for directing our spiritual lives, so that we might live a more fulfilling and godly life in Christ.

As we pursue this godliness, we must come to understand as well as embrace the manifold dimensions of God. God is all-knowing. God is all-powerful. He is all-sufficient. And it is out of this sufficiency that the all-powerful God created the heavens and the earth.

The formation of the heavens and the earth was not formulated from brick and mortar or from some other tangible source; rather it was created by the Word of God.

A careful examination of this advent will not only illuminate the reality of the power of God, but it will reveal the dimension of power that was comprised in the words (voice) of God.

The voice of God is powerful. The voice of God is mighty. The voice of God is awesome. And the voice of God is authority.

There are two words in the Greek for power: *dunamis and exousia.* Dunamis means ability and might. Exousia means freedom of action, right to act, absolute and unrestricted.

A police officer is a good example of both of these words being portrayed. A police officer has *exousia* – the right to detain and arrest people; and he also has *dunamis* – firearm, the power to shoot people. God exercised both of these powers in creating the heavens and the earth.

All power (dunamis) and authority (exousia) belongs to Him. But what makes the creation so unique outside of the creation itself, is that it was created by words. It was God's voice that created the worlds – *"And God said."* The Psalmist says it this way when referring to the power in the voice of God:

"The voice of the Lord is upon the
waters: the God of glory
thundereth: the Lord is upon many
waters.

The voice of the Lord is powerful;
the voice of the Lord is full of
majesty.

The voice of the Lord breaketh the cedars; yea, the Lord breaketh the cedars of Lebanon...

The voice of the Lord divideth the flames of fire.

The voice of the Lord shaketh the wilderness...

The voice of the Lord maketh the hinds to calve, and discovereth the forests..."

Psalm 29:3-9

A Voice Activation Kingdom

In Genesis, we are introduced to the systematic approach of which God chose to create the heaven and the earth. The thing that is pungent within the text is the channel God chose to release change into the earth. It was through **"words"** he chose to create – *"And God said...and it was so"*-- and the heavens and earth were formed. It was His voice and His words that vibrated with power that caused the elements in the cosmic world to come into alignment. This is a powerful implication of the significance of words.

Whatever God said, it came to pass. His words created what He said. When He spoke, His words created a chain of events to take place. A critical explanation of the text, then lends itself to the conclusion that the voice of God is an ACTIVATION resource. In other words, the establishment of change can be activated by words in the kingdom of God. One evangelist said it this way, "Any time God wanted to change someone's life, He always touched their mouth." The mouth is an intricate component, which God has always utilized to release change.

When God spoke, things immediately were manifested. The Word of God was spoken *first* before it was written. However, it was written to be spoken.

The Establishment of a Law

The book of Genesis is a book of beginnings. It is the origin of all things. As the book of Genesis unfolds, each beginning establishes a principle or law that governs future actions. When something is done for the first time in scripture, it comes under the heading of the *Law of First Mention.* Meaning, from this point on, whenever someone desires to do something based on a previous encounter, then in order to get the same results, then he or she has to do the same thing(s) that was done previously to get the same results. Bottom line: He or she would have to emulate the action(s) that brought about the result.

According to Genesis, we are made in the likeness and image of God; therefore, we are an exact copy of God (Genesis 1:26). For some, this might "ruffle some feathers." But this is what *"image"* mean in this verse. But hold on, let me clarify.

We are told in verse 26, that we are made in the image and likeness of God. Image and likeness are two different words. Therefore, they have two different meanings.

Likeness means state or quality of being like, similarity, facsimile, something that is like. What is God like? What are His attributes? What are the characteristics of God?

God is love, pure, holy, honest, righteous, merciful, sovereign, kind, and compassionate. God is also truth. These are just some of the attributes of God. So we, as believers, should be like (emulate) these traits.

Now, let's examine the word "image." The word image means a representation of a person or thing, drawn, painting; the visual impression of something produced by a mirror; a copy, and a type. These are some pretty strong and descriptive definitions.

While we are not God, it is cited that we were made in the "image" and "likeness" of Him. Therefore, we should have characteristics like God **and** we should also be able to exercise authority in this earth like God.

From the beginning of time we (the creation), were designed like our creator. We were an exact image of God. We walked like God. We talked like God. We had His DNA.

However, sin disrupted our likeness and image of God so for a period of time we had a warped state. But thank God for Jesus. He redeemed us back to our original state (place with God) by His blood.

"In whom we have redemption through his blood, even the forgiveness of sins:

Who is the image of the invisible God, the firstborn of every creature:

For by him were all things created, that are in heaven, and that are in earth, visible and invisible, whether they be thrones, or dominions, or principalities, or powers: all things were created by him, and for him:

And he is before all things, and by
him all things consist."

Colossians 1:14-17

So now, we can operate again from our original blueprint (form) instead of out of our fallen nature. Our original blueprint affords us the ability to create things with our voices just as God did. Your voice is your address now in the realm of the spirit.

What we (the body of Christ) must realize is that the kingdom of God *truly* is a voice activation kingdom. It is a kingdom governed by words and framed by words – *"Through faith we understand that the worlds were framed by the word of God, so that the things which are seen were not made of things which do appear"* (Hebrews 11:3).

Some scientists say that our voice can accurately identify us like a fingerprint. The invisible world will always supersede the visible world. God works in the invisible realm; therefore, we must operate out of the same realm if we expect the same outcome as the Father. Yes, today, the body of Christ has the same authority to manifest in this manner.

God's voice was His agent of change; therefore, our voice is the agent of change. His words framed the worlds, so our words can frame or create our world as well. Our voice is a key element that God uses to activate the miraculous in our lives.

Death and Life Are In Your Mouth

Proverbs 18:20-21 says, "A man's belly shall be *satisfied* with the fruit of his mouth; and with the increase of his lips shall he be filled. Death and life are in the power of the tongue: and they that love it shall eat the fruit thereof."

Have you ever wondered why some people seem more blessed than others? Their lives look much easier and more carefree. One of the reasons, I believe, is that with their mouths, they speak more positive things.

Our conversation reveals whether we are winners or losers, successful or failures.

Some people speak more negative things over their lives, than others. Some people speak more positive things over their lives than others. Let me ask you, who do you think would have a more fulfilling and enriched life? The people who speak more negative things or positive things? Of course, the people who speak more positive things will have a more fulfilling life.

Our conversation reveals whether we are winners or losers, successful or failures -- "Out of the abundance of the heart the mouth speaketh" (Matthew 12:34). Losers focus on their problems; winners focus on their possibilities. Losers major on obstacles, but winners major on opportunities.

Death and life are truly in the power of our tongue. The words we speak can be constructive and/or destructive. This is why we need to monitor carefully the words that come out of our mouths. Proverbs 18:6-8 says, *"A fool's lips enter into contention, and his mouth calleth for strokes. A fool's mouth is his destruction, and his lips are the snare of his soul. The words of a talebearer are as wounds, and they go down into the innermost parts of the belly."*

The words we speak have a unique potential to destroy or build up. If you don't believe it, just compliment someone today and watch the response. I guarantee you will see immediately a change in that person's countenance.

You either are going to ask for what you want or settle for what you get.

Our voices and words are mighty forces in the universe. Everything in our lives revolves around and involves words. Words are an intricate part of our communication media. Whether we're at work, at home, at church, or in the grocery store, words are a part of the equation.

If you speak blessings and kind words, then you will receive blessings and kind words in return. If you speak negative and evil words, then you will receive negative and evil words in return. It is called the law of reciprocity. According to the scriptures, it is called sowing and reaping.

If you sow death, you will reap death. If you sow life, you will reap life. If you want a more fulfilling and enriched life, then you have to create the world you want with your mouth. It is not your boss' fault. It is not your girlfriend's fault. It is not your wife's or husband's fault that your life is not the way you want it. It is your fault. You have to create your own world with *your* words -- *"Through faith we understand that the worlds were framed by the word of God...."*

Are You Settling

You either are going to ask for what you want or settle for what you get. Mark 11:23-24 say, *"For verily I say unto you, that whosoever shall **say** unto this mountain, Be thou removed, and be thou cast into the sea; and shall not doubt in his heart, but shall believe that those things which he **saith** shall come to pass; he shall have whatsoever he **saith**. Therefore I say unto you, what things soever ye desire, when ye pray, believe that ye receive them, and ye shall have them."*

Be wise and make every word you speak count toward building a bright and positive future for you.

If you don't like the world you have created for yourself, then change it. Otherwise, you will be settling − *"I call heaven and earth to record this day against you, that I have set before you life and death,* blessing and cursing: therefore choose life, that both thou and thy seed may live" (Deuteronomy 30:19). So if you want your world to change, change what you are saying. Choose life! Choose words that will release life into your life -- words that have the ability to go beyond the mind and enter directly into the heart of mankind.

Whatever we say with our mouth daily releases vibrations into the cosmic realm whereby the universe seeks to create them. Therefore, the sooner you start saying the things you want; the sooner the universe will begin to align up to bring it to pass. This is what Mark 11:23-24 is saying, we can have what we say. A man by the name of Solomon Gabirol said once, *"I can retract what I did not say, but I cannot retract what I already have said."*

Today, if you have been just settling for what you have, then I want to challenge you, today, to begin to etch out a new path for your life! Someone once wrote, that your future does not respond to anyone else's voice but yours. Be wise and make every word you speak count toward building a bright and positive future for you. *"For by thy words thou shalt be justified, and by thy words thou shalt be condemned"* (Matthew 12:37).

It is said that there are three types of people on planet earth: museum keepers, settlers, and pioneers.

- Museum keepers are people who are content with walking down memory lane, looking at the past only.
- Settlers are people who stay in their comfort zone; they don't like change.
- Pioneers are people who are constantly changing and pressing into new territories; they are courageous.

Today, you need to make up in your mind which one you are going to become. Are you going to be a museum keeper, just constantly talking about, "I remember when..." Or are you going to be a settler, never wanting to venture out and do something new. Or finally, do you want to be a pioneer, someone who is constantly looking for the greatness of God to be manifested in his or her life. If I were you, I would strive to be a pioneer. To be honest, if you are going to receive all that God has for you in this life, you *have* to be a pioneer. God is forever etching out new paths in life, and we have to be open for the "**new**" of God.

Old wine skin cannot hold new wine – *"Neither do men put new wine into old bottles: else the bottles break, and the wine runneth out, and the bottles perish: but they put new wine into new bottles, and both are preserved"* (Matthew 9:17).

Our minds have to be renewed and opened to the newness of God if we are going to have what we say.

If you want something new from God, then you have to do something you never done before. Unless there is a new you, there will not be a new you!!!

Chapter 2

THINK BIG
(God Will Do What He Said)

"For as he thinketh in his heart, so is he...."

Proverbs 23:7

Everything begins in the mind! Before we act upon something, a thought precedes it. All actions are governed by a thought. It is said this way: a thought brings about an action. An action fosters a behavior. A behavior facilitates a habit. And a habit renders a destiny. So is our thinking important to our success in life? You better believe it.

The mind is the seat of the master puppetry. Whoever or whatever controls the mind will dictate its future. Therefore, harnessing your thoughts is extremely critical to your life's dreams and destinies coming to pass. If we can master our thoughts, we can master our future. Our future success depends upon us thinking correctly.

The human spirit is a rich soil. What is planted within it, will grow, *unless,* there is an interruption in its path. One great scientist said, "A thing will stay in motion until it is interrupted by something else."

We have to guard our minds at all times. For some, this is difficult because they are already "damaged" goods. They grew up in homes that told them, "They will never be anything." "They are going to be like this person or that person." "You won't mount to nothing." "They would never have enough."

When we grow up in negative environments such as these, our worldview is tainted. We grow up from being negative and inferior children to negative and inferior adults.

Our belief systems are warped as well, so when we get saved, we have a difficult time believing God wants to bless our lives.

Other people's challenge when growing up was their concept about money. Boy!!!...do some of you have the wrong concept about money, and this is especially true in the church. Some people were told, "They can never get ahead," "They are never going to get the job they want," "They are doomed to be poor," "They are never going to make it in life," and "Money don't grow on trees." If you heard these things repeatedly growing up in life, then these things created a negative belief system in your mind regarding success and money. In other words, you have a predisposition to developing a poverty mentality.

A poverty mentality is an attitude. It is a way of thinking that is said to perpetuate poverty because the focus is on what a person does not have rather than what he or she does have.

Do You Have A Poverty Mentality?

If there is ever an enemy to our success, it is operating out of a poverty mentality. A poverty mentality is a tremendous stronghold, which is designed to keep you in bondage. And it can last for generations.

According to research, a poverty mentality is an attitude. It is a way of thinking that is said to perpetuate poverty because the focus is on what a person does not have rather than what he or she does have. Thoughts and statements such as "I can't afford this..." and "I'll never have enough money for that..." can be a self-fulfilling prophecy.

Furthermore, it is a spirit that conspires to trap people in a cycle of poor choices and slavery to money. But it doesn't stop here. It is also known for its power to afflict poor people. It afflicts the human heart so much that it produces a generation of poverty mentality people. This spirit is one of the main causes that poor people pursue money apart from creating value. Additionally, generational poverty has its own culture, hidden rules and belief systems.

Essentially, generational poverty is an attitude of a destructive mindset to a person and a generation of self-belief empowerment rather than one of self-pity and jealousy.

As you study up on the poverty mentality, you will discover that there are two types of poverties that need to be addressed: Situational and Generational.

Situational poverty is a period of poverty caused by situational factors. A number of things can cause situational poverty to occur: divorce, loss of job, death of a spouse, and unexpected expenses. These uncontrollable events can cause a chain of events which can lead to a *period* of situational poverty.

In contrast, generational poverty is a form of entrenched poverty which can encompass multiple generations of a family. If poverty has existed at least two generations in a family lineage, the supposition here is that the members of the family are preprogrammed to have poverty mentalities.

One writer wrote, "It is important to recognize this time factor to be able to separate it from 'situational poverty,' characteristically understood as a lack of resources due to particular sets of events, i.e. a death, chronic illness, divorce, etc. from the discussion of generational poverty." These two concepts are distinguishable, which assists in putting people's behavior in better perspective. A key indicator in defining and separating these poverty types is "attitude." In generational poverty, the players feel that society owes them a living whereas in situational, they often allow pride to keep them from accepting needed assistance.

Jesus Cursed the Fig Tree

The story in the book of Mark, Chapter 11 talks about how Jesus was hungry one day and from a distance, He saw a fig tree and assumed this fig tree would satisfy His hunger. However, when he arrived at the tree, there was no fruit. Because it did not have any fruit, Jesus cursed it and said, "No man eat fruit of thee hereafter for ever." And the next morning when Jesus and His disciples passed by this tree, it had dried up from the root.

This is a very interesting narrative regarding the power to curse and destroy things at its root. If you don't like the fruit of something in your life, then you must get to the root of the problem. The fruit will always reflect its roots. Why is this important? Because many of the problems some of us are dealing with are generational. We were told things that were not necessarily true. As well, we saw behaviors that reinforced these things. So inadvertently, poverty mentalities have developed. And these negative thought patterns have destroyed many lives.

Jesus came that we might have life and have it more abundantly – *"I am come that they might have life, and that they might have it more abundantly"* (John 10:10). In order for some of us to walk out this abundant life, we have to curse some things in our past – things in our generational bloodline.

Abundant life or abundant living is not being "broke" all the time. It is not being down and out. It is not being a beggar and borrower. This is not the life God has for His people!

We are the sole architect of our own future. How we think about things will determine our destiny.

It is hard for some people to see themselves prosperous and successful. A lot of this has to do with the image in their mind and words spoken over their lives. This poverty mentality has shaped their mindsets. To uproot these erroneous thoughts or destroy them, they have to dismantle all the words and mindsets that have been spoken over their lives in the past.

"(For the weapons of our warfare are not carnal, but mighty through God to the pulling down of strong holds;)

Casting down imaginations, and every high thing that exalteth itself against the knowledge of God, and bringing into captivity every thought to the obedience of Christ" (II Corinthians 10:4-5).

Pulling down these strongholds in our minds is not always an easy task, but if you want change badly enough, then you will do what it will take to see change. You see, change does not begin externally; it begins internally. It begins in the mind. Ten percent of life is what happens to us, and ninety percent is how we respond to it. We are the sole architect of our own future. How we think about things will determine our destiny.

The mind is always cross-examining the revelation of the Spirit of God in us. But be assured, God does not play mind games with our future. What God does in the spirit is greater than what's happening in our minds. God is clear about what He wants for His children. The prophet Jeremiah says it this way, *"For I know the thoughts that I think toward you, saith the Lord, thoughts of peace, and not of evil, to give you an expected end"* -- other translations say, *"to give you a future and a hope."* Just so you know, the enemy of our future is always resistant to change. The devil does **not** want us to succeed. Dr. Mike Murdock, a 21st century wisdom leader, says, *"Men do not decide their future; they decide their habits that determine their future."*

Successful people have daily habits and they are known for having a great deal of self-discipline. Before Mary Kay Ash of Mary Kay Cosmetics became ill and died, she would arise daily and write down her top six priorities. She was extremely successful in the cosmetic industry.

We have to create habits that emulate success, so that we can receive all that God has for us. God is not a man that He should lie (Numbers 23:19). Whatever He said He will do, He will do it. The problem is not with God, it is with us. It is with our minds. So the first place we must begin to change our world is with our minds. And if we have been operating out of a poverty mentality, then we have to retrain our minds to think right! Remember, we are the architect of our thoughts. We have to cultivate our minds to function more positively. We need the right side and left side of our brain to be congruent. We have to think correspondingly.

In James Allen's book, *As A Man Thinketh*, he says, "A man's mind may be likened to a garden, which may be intelligently cultivated or allowed to run wild; but whether cultivated or neglected, it must, and will, bring forth." He also says, "Until thought is linked with purpose there is no intelligent accomplishment."

"The strongest and dominate thoughts that satiate our minds will be the direction we will be guided toward. That which controls us is that which masters our thoughts. It is absolutely essential that we dismantle erroneous thoughts and misconceptions that are plaguing our minds. If not, our destiny will be thwarted. Our destiny will be aborted or an illegitimate destiny will come forth," according to Dr.

Shirley Clark, a motivational speaker and prolific author.

We have to learn to weed out and keep weeding out until no more residue of the previous mindset exists within our mind. Once we do this, we can then reach the target of our aspirations. Proverbs 23:7 says, *"For as he thinketh in his heart, so is he...."*

Breaking the cycle of generational poverty

Generational poverty is a stronghold. A stronghold is classified as a strong defense, a fortress. Something that is hard to penetrate. Because of the protracted amount of time, generational poverty might have been in a family for years. Dismantling or destroying this spirit can be very challenging to overcome. Some people never recover or come out. However, here are some things that were outlined in my research that people can do to dismantle a poverty mentality.

1. <u>Investing time in being a life-long learner</u>.

Read, Read, Read! If you want to defeat a poverty mentality, you have to renew your mind. The older folks used to say, "An idle mind is the devil's work ground." Ecclesiastes, chapter 10 and verse 18 says, *"By much slothfulness the building decayeth; and through idleness of the hands the house droppeth through."* You have to fill your mind with new information when dismantling old information. You have to read books, magazines, articles, etc. -- any enrichment and empowerment information will help dismantle previous "programming." If you were told, you would never amount to anything, then you want to read information that is contrary to this programming. I will share more about developing your mind in chapter five.

2. <u>Being in poverty is rarely about a lack of intelligence or your ability.</u>

One of the misconceptions about a poverty mentality is that only poor (financially challenged) people have a poverty mentality. This is not true. Remember, a poverty mentality has more to do with an attitude and belief systems than the amount of money you have. So you can come from a family that was well off financially, but still believe, money is evil. Or you might have come from a family that focuses on pending financial loss or financial disaster that they spend most of their time hording their money and afraid constantly of being homeless. And the problem here is that they spend most of their time focusing on being homeless instead of enjoying their wealth. Basically, this is a fear of failure that has paralyzed them. Many intelligent and talented people have a poverty mentality.

3.   <u>People stay in poverty because they do not see a way out.</u>

Not everybody wants to stay in poverty. However, some people just don't know how to get out. Nor do they know how to access the resources or information to assist with their exodus. This is why I am writing this book, to help people like this. I want to make sure that everyone knows that he or she can make it. They don't have to stay in their situation.   They can live a victorious life. They just have to believe what the Word of God says about their situation and walk it out. You are an overcomer!

Bottom line: Your future can be promising or painful, depending on the routines you have established in your life and how you think about things.

> *"Finally, brethren, whatsoever things are true, whatsoever things are honest, whatsoever things are just, whatsoever things are pure,*

*whatsoever things are lovely, whatsoever things are of good report: if there be any virtue, and if there be any praise, **think** on these things."*

Philippians 4:8

Chapter 3

DREAM BIG
(GOD MAKES DREAMS POSSIBLE)

"For a dream cometh through the multitude of business; and a fool's voice is known by multitude of words."

Ecclesiastes 5:3

How big can you dream? How big is your imagination? No matter how big your dream or imagination is, God's dream and imagination is bigger. There is a song and some of the lyrics are *"To Dream the Impossible Dream."* While this is a beautiful song, it is not for Christians who know their God – *"He that knoweth his God shall be strong and do great exploits"* (Daniel 11:32). With God, according to the scripture, all things are possible -- *"The things which are impossible with men are possible with God"* (Luke 18:27).

Men who dreamed great dreams have been men who became builders of great things and did great things.

People who dream big often achieve big things. Anybody can think small. But can you dream big? Can you imagine yourself doing things that are beyond your limitations? If money were not an object, how big could you dream?

Men who dreamed great dreams have been men who became builders of great things and did great things: designed large buildings, wrote the Constitution and flew the first airplane.

Wealth begins in the mind. You have to expand your mind beyond your present to receive the wealth of the land. There must be a constant compass inside of your mind pointing you toward your success and your destiny.

One writer wrote, "Every great achievement is conceived first through a dream." When we study the scriptures, God used dreams many times to give men direction and guidance about their future, destiny and potential:

- King Abimelech – God showed King Abimelech in a dream that his life was coming to an end if he slept with Abraham's wife, Sarah (Genesis 20:3)

- Nebuchadnezzar – Because of Nebuchadnezzar's rebellion, God showed him in a dream the destruction that was coming upon his life (Daniel 2:3)

- Daniel – God showed Daniel in a dream, events that were going to happen upon the earth. (Daniel 7)

- Joseph – God showed Joseph in a

dream   about   Mary's   pregnancy.
(Matthew 1:20)

"If you don't have a dream how are you going to make a dream come true"--Oscar Hammerstein--

Joseph, the Dreamer

I love the story in the book of Genesis (Chapters 37-39) about Joseph, and how God showed him in a dream that he was going to be a ruler in Egypt. However, when we are introduced to this story, it looked like everything but this. In fact, it starts off being a story about abandonment, betrayal, hate, deceit and disappointment. It was a story about how Joseph was afflicted with an incredible amount of pain and anguish at the hands of his brothers. But here is the clincher; it was all because he had a dream.

Here is the story: Joseph had a dream one night about how his brothers' sheaves were bowing down to his sheaves. When he told his brothers about the dream, they became incensed. The scripture said they hated him the more. They said, "Shalt thou indeed reign over us?"

On another night, Joseph had a second dream, but this time he told his father and brothers. And the scriptures said the brothers became even more enraged, so much so that they plotted his murder. First, they threw him into a pit, and then, they sold him to the Ishmaelites in Egypt. Despite all that his brothers did to him, Joseph did not lose hope. Because of Joseph's attitude he did not get bitter about his situation, and the Bible said God was with him – *"And Joseph was brought down to Egypt...and the Lord was with Joseph"* (Genesis 39:1-2).

This statement alone will preach. No matter how bad our situation is, if we would understand that God is always with us, then we are going to come out on top. This is what happened to Joseph in Egypt. The dream that he dreamed came to pass in Egypt. In the least expected place, God brought his dream to pass. Joseph became second in command in Pharaoh's house. And during this era, Pharaoh was the governor of Egypt.

How many times have we thought that we had to be with a certain person, in a certain place or everything has to line up in order for God to bless us? I have good news, if you thought or think this way. These are not prerequisites to God blessing you. The only thing that invokes change is that God be with you. The key to Joseph's success was that he never forgot about his dream. He never forgot what God had promised him.

If you are going to be successful in life, you have to keep dreaming. You have to dream big and you have to dream long. For every dream you dream, there is a day for the fulfillment of this dream. Great things are given to those who dream. We have to dream big, now. We have to fight against these mediocre and average thoughts and see the big picture. Yes! Is it going to be tough at times? Yes! Is it going to be challenging at times? Yes! You will be misunderstood at times. But you must persevere no matter what. You must endure at all cost. *Endurance* in the Greek means to be left standing when all else has collapsed.

Joseph could have given up many times. But he did not. Besides being sold into slavery by his siblings, he was falsely accused of raping his boss' wife, and because of this, he served a prison sentence for two years. Just because a prophetic word was spoken over your life that you are going to do great things, does not mean it is going to be easy. In fact, I submit to you that because you do have a great destiny, you are going to have a great deal of warfare. Your destiny determines your warfare!

Dream Killers/Dream Makers

Watch out for dream killers! The people we associate with are either going to make us or break us. Some people are negative by nature and have pessimistic attitudes. They never see anything in a positive way. They are constantly looking for the "hammer to fall." These are the types of people we should not be hanging around. They are dream killers.

Also, some people will hate you just because you have a dream. Their lives are so mundane that they cannot see beyond their current problems, so they hate you for having a vision. In addition, sometimes your vision can be so big that other people cannot possibly comprehend that God wants to do this for you. Therefore, instead of embracing and encouraging you, they will reject you.

Not everybody is happy with what God is doing or wants to do for you. This was so true in Joseph's situation. Dream killers, they are on assignment from the devil. In the book, *Warring With Your Prophetic Word,* the author says it this way:

> *The devil will always have dream killers to demise or ridicule what God is doing in your life. Listen to what Joseph's brothers said when they saw him coming toward them – "And they said one to another, Behold, **this dreamer cometh**" (Genesis 37:19). Can't you hear the disdain in this statement?*

Dreamers are possibility thinkers and dream killers are impossibility thinkers. You see the difference between a dreamer and a dream killer is that a dreamer sees their dream as a reality in their spirit way before it is ever manifested in the natural. And a dream killer can never see beyond its own negative experiences and unfulfilled desires. This is why it is hard to persuade a dreamer to forget about a dream when his mind is made up. You see, a God-given dream is hard to shake off because images of the dream are constantly being played repeatedly inside their spirit and mind.

So no matter what happened to Joseph in the interim to his destiny, he used his dream as the compass for staying on course. No matter what his family thought about him. No matter what

Potiphar's wife said about him. Joseph's success was based on his identification with God and not how others defined him. Thirteen years Joseph encountered repeated negative experiences, but he never lost faith in God's goodness. And because he didn't, he prospered. Remember: Nobody on earth can make you feel inferior without your permission. God's purpose will always take everything that you have ever gone through or going through to develop your full potential. This is why Joseph could declare at the end of the matter, "But as for you, ye thought evil against me: but God meant it unto good..." (Genesis 50:20).

In the book, *Keys to Receiving Your Miracles*, by Guy Peh, we have two types of people in our lives: good people and bad people.

Good people will encourage your dream, will stir up your dream, will sow seed in your life, and will challenge you to go higher with God. On the other hand, bad people will kill your dream, will pull you down, will cause you to backslide, and will encourage you to walk in vices. Make sure you surround your life with good people instead of bad people.

Never accept failure when

you have a dream.

The Power to Achieve

According to another prolific author and leadership trainer, John Maxwell, "The difference between average people and achieving people is their perception of and response to failure." He believes that in order for an individual to endure opposition, there must be a sense of purpose. How we view adversity and failure is determined by what lenses we are looking through. If we are looking through lenses of doubt and fear, then we are going to see doom and gloom. If we are looking through the lenses of purpose and destiny, then we are going to see success and fulfillment. How we prosper in life has a lot to do with how we handle adversity.

Adversity should always be looked at as a stepping stone to advancement. And setbacks should always be looked at as stepping stones to success. Never accept failure when you have a dream. You see, the dream will be the thing that will empower you so that you can keep on going.

So what? One way did not work; try another way. If you can conceive it, you can achieve it. *"And the Lord said, behold, the people is one, and they have all one language; and this they begin to do; **and now nothing will be restrained from them, which they have imagined to do"** (Genesis 11:6).

According to Dr. Shirley Clark, again, a prolific author and international motivational speaker, "The power to achieve is inside all of us. But it is what we do with this power that is the demarcation of whether you are successful or not. Purpose is a success factor. This is why the need to discover our purpose is invaluable. When purpose is defined and pursued, success is inevitable. However, success is always a process. And it is the process we often want to forfeit. Our road to success is usually comprised of numerous accounts of failures and mistakes. This is why the process to purpose is not always palatable. I am reminded of a statement in John Maxwell's book, *Falling Forward.* "We must give ourselves permission to fail and permission to excel."

Developing a Millionaire Mentality

Dreaming big is a part of millionaires' nature. It is a common attribute among them. In the book, *Secrets of the Millionaire Mind,* it states that millionaires don't talk about their jobs, they talk about wealth. They talk in terms of their greatness or worth versus poor people (financially challenged/people with jobs), who talk about what type of job they have or what salary they want to make.

Rich people deal with net worth, not working income. According to millionaires, the true measure of wealth is not working income; it is net worth. From a rich person's standpoint, income is just one of the components in your net worth. There are savings. There are investments. There are insurances. Several other things are factored in when they talk about wealth. But unfortunately, poor and middle-class people are only accustomed to talking about working income. Rich people think big, poor people think small.

Now, when I talk about the difference between rich people and poor people, I am not trying to make poor people feel bad about their situation. My goal is to challenge poor people to think differently about their lives. I want to challenge them in their thinking, so that they will know that they can make it in life, and that they can be delivered from poverty.

Millionaire Myron Golden was a trash man before he became a millionaire. He used to sit in garbage trucks at stop lights reading books on financial success and self-help. He read so much that it changed his situation. So no matter what situation you are in, you don't have to stay there. You just have to make up in your mind that you want to change.

Do You Value Yourself?

Thinking big has a lot to do with knowing your value. If you devalue yourself and think small about your gifts and talents, then you are thinking too small. If you value your worth, then others will value your worth. But if you devalue your worth, then others will devalue your worth. Today, you need to make up in your mind if you are going to play with the big leagues or the little leagues. I like what Dr. Phil McGraw, who is a well known talk show host, says, "We teach people how to treat us by our actions."

If you want people to treat you a certain way, then you have to communicate this to them whether verbal or nonverbal. We must be the sign to show people how we want to be treated.

According to the author of the *Secrets of the Millionaire Mind*, he says that most people choose to play small. He said there are two reasons they do this: fear of failure and feeling small.

Fear of failure will always be part of the equation. It is what you do with this fear that determines your outcome. We all are faced with obstacles at times, but we cannot allow fear to overtake us and thwart our progress. Successful people look fear in the face and persevere no matter what.

Also, never define failure as a self-worth issue. If you do, your present state will be rejection and despondency. Always define it as a learning tool; then your outlook on life will be more positive. You will have a winning attitude.

Never *ever* attach failure to your self-worth or value. The sum total or worth of whom you are should not be judged solely on your status. The worth of whom you are is determined by your character and what God says about you.

Feeling small...get over it! You have to know you have value if you are going to make a difference in this world. Too many people are focused on themselves too much. Successful people solve other people's problems. The world is bigger than you, so see the bigger picture. There is something inside of you that the world needs. Believe in yourself, look up and not down. According to one great philosopher, "The purpose of our lives is to add value to the people of this generation and those that follow." Are you a good leader?

God Wants You Wealthy

Okay, I know when we talk about wealth, money and God in the same sentence, some people get a little uneasy, but God will not get mad at us for being wealthy. If this were so, why did He give Abraham and Solomon in the Bible so much wealth?

Abraham: "And Abram was *very* rich in cattle, in silver, and in gold." (Genesis 13:2)

Solomon: "So King Solomon *exceeded* all the kings of the earth for riches and for wisdom." (I Kings 10:23)

Many people have a problem with the statement that God wants us wealthy. However, if we were to ask most people, do they want more money, they would say, yes. Or why can't they do this or that? It most likely will be because they do not have enough money. Well, if this is true, it seems to me you would be open to hear about how to receive more, than being upset about the idea that God wants you rich.

Personally, I know what is going on inside of your mind -- stinking thinking! You have been taught wrong. This goes back to chapter two. Your previous programming about money, the Bible, church and God was erroneous. And you are not convinced yet, so let's look at what the Bible says about money. Then I will address erroneous doctrine or teaching about money. You see, if you are going to have what God said you can have, then you have to know what God said you can have. Also, I will be addressing the poverty mentality where you feel you don't deserve to be wealthy.

In the book, *Welcome to a Winner's World,* it talks about 10 lies people believe about money. I am not going to expound on all of them, but here is the list:

1. Money is unimportant
2. Money is evil
3. Money never hurt anyone
4. Money will cure most problems and ensure happiness
5. Some are gifted for wealth and some are destined for poverty
6. God doesn't want you to have money
7. There is nothing you can do about your financial situation
8. Regularity of giving and amount are not important to God
9. Money is an unscriptural subject and not to be discussed in church

10. It is selfish and wrong to give expecting to receive in return

As you can see, this is a wonderful list, but for the sake of this discourse, I am only going to deal with four of these statements: 2, 5, 6 and 9.

First, I want to address number two: Money is evil. Money is not evil; money is neutral. Money is neither good nor bad. The owners of the money are the only people that these characteristics can be attached to, not the money. Often we misquote the scripture in the Bible that says, "For the *love* of money is the root of all evil" (I Timothy 6:10). As we can see, money is not the problem; the love of money is the problem. Let's keep this scripture in context.

I agree there are a lot of abuse and misuse of money, but money is not evil in itself. For example, fire when not controlled can damage a lot of property. But when controlled, it can be used to cook a wonderful gourmet meal. It is all about managing it.

Second, I wish to address number five: Some are gifted for wealth and some are destined for poverty. Deuteronomy 8:18, is an excellent scripture to outwit this lie. "But thou shalt remember the Lord thy God: *for it is he that giveth thee power to get wealth,* that he may establish his covenant which he sware unto thy fathers, as it is this day."

God is the one who is giving us the power to get wealth -- not I, not the preacher, not your pastor, but God.

Now, if God gives us power to attain wealth, then God has given all of us the potential to get wealthy. So what is the problem in our obtaining our wealth? Glad you asked! God is only going to give us the "power" (the energy, the idea, the vision), then we have to work the plan.

Miracles rarely happen to those living in the status quo.

Okay, this is where the "rubber meets the road." Some people are going to do more than others to see their dreams come to pass. Let's face it, some people are lazy. This is why some people have more than others. And it has nothing to do with whether God wants you wealthy or not. But I really want to address this lazy spirit. Here's what the scriptures have to say about lazy people:

HARD WORK:
"In all labour there is profit: but the talk of the lips tendeth only to penury." (Proverbs 14:23).

"Hard work means prosperity, only a fool idles away his time." (Proverbs 12:11LB).

"For even when we were with you, this we commanded you, that if any would not work, neither should he eat" (II Thessalonians 3:10).

Basically, Proverbs is saying talk is cheap. **All** labor will bring some kind of profit. The key word here is *"all."* If you work hard, you will prosper. It's time to get busy!

Even if you are on the right track, you'll get run over if you just sit there.

I can hear your voices now, "I do work hard and I am still broke." I admonish you to go back and read chapter two. You might get some more insight on your situation. There are two things you should never do with time: waste time or kill time. Time is a precious commodity. You can never get it back once it is gone. Make every minute count toward your destiny.

DILIGENT PERSON:

"He becometh poor that dealeth with a slack hand: but the hand of the diligent maketh rich." (Proverbs 10:4)

"Always poor is he who works with an indolent hand, but the hand of the diligent brings wealth." (Proverbs 10:4ML)

"Lazy men are soon poor, hard workers get rich." (Proverbs 10:4LB)

"A slack hand causes poverty, but the hand of the diligent makes rich." (Proverbs **10:4**(RS)

I wanted you to read this scripture in the different versions of the Bible, so it will make an impact. We are either going to be poor or rich by *"our"* hands -- not by God's hands. So if we are broke, it is not God's fault; it is our fault. We have to tap into the created side of God to find our wealth stream — *"...it is God who giveth us power to get wealth."*

Miracles rarely happen to those living in the status quo.

SLUGGISH PERSON:

"The soul of the sluggard desireth, and hath nothing: but the soul of the diligent shall be made fat." (Proverbs 13:4)

"A sluggard will not plow for reason of the cold, therefore shall he begin harvest, and have nothing." (Proverbs 20:4)

"Go to the ant, thou sluggard; consider her ways, and be wise: which having no guide, overseer, or ruler, provideth her meat in the summer, and gathereth her food in the harvest. How long wilt thou sleep, O sluggard...So shall thy poverty come as one that traveleth, and thy want as an armed man." (Proverbs 6:6-11)

Wow...what an incredible analogy! If you are lazy and lethargic in any aspect of your life right now, I hope these scriptures will motivate you to get up and do. Your travail will be hard and your wants will be like an armed man if you don't get up. It's going to be very difficult for you to be successful in this state. You got to get up and get in an activation manifestation state. Even if you are on the right track, you'll get run over if you just sit there. Faith without works is dead (James 2:20).

In addition, God explains that financial curses and blessings are also due to our obedience to the Word of God. "Blessed shall thou be or cursed, shall you be..." (Deuteronomy, Chapter 28). The book of Malachi also addresses blessings in chapter three where we learn about giving to God what is rightly His (tithes and offerings), so that we might receive a blessing so large we will not have room to receive it.

Next, I want to deal with number six: God does not want you to have money. If anyone has half a brain, you know that this statement is crazy. We live in a world that revolves around money and the exchange of it. Our daily livelihood depends on using money to meet our basic needs in life (water, lights, rent, clothing, food, etc.), so this statement is just only a ploy to keep people in poverty by the devil. God gives us power to get wealth (Deuteronomy 28); He is a provider (Matthew 7:9), and according to Ecclesiastes 10:19, money answers all things. If money answers all things, then God wants us to have money more than just to pay our bills.

Finally, number nine: Money is an unscriptural subject and it is not to be discussed in the church. If there has been ever a lie told to the church, this is one. This is ridiculous! The Bible is filled with scriptures addressing money and how to handle it. I just listed quite a few of them. What we have to do is stop reading things into the scripture, but rather read out of the scripture.

Often we confer or project information into the Word of God when we are reading it that the text is not saying. Why do we do this? Because of our upbringing -- what we were programmed to see. The Bible is filled with warnings and many promises regarding money, riches and wealth. A lot of this teaching, though, comes out of the "prosperity gospel" teaching, so let's look at this.

The Prosperity Gospel

At the conclusion of this section, I want us to look at some of the scriptures, preachers, missionaries and theologians often use to tell people God does not want them rich. Right now, for some people, I would be considered a prosperity preacher or preaching the prosperity gospel. This is why; I have intentionally only given you the Word of God, so you can see the truth for yourself. You be the judge. Not my own opinion, just the Word of God.

This is what we are supposed to do - give the Word of God to you and you search it out. If you come to a conclusion, after you have searched it out, that I am wrong, then stick with what you have proven in the Word. At least you would have done your homework. And hurray for you, you are in the minority!

Now, let's get back on track. As I delve into the subject why some people feel we need to be broke, I want you to know there are several thoughts about this subject.

Some groups or sects are so adamant about being poor that they have taken poverty vows thinking this will make them more holy. They sell everything they have and eat out of garbage cans. The poorest man is not the one without a penny, but he who is without a dream. This is so true.

Many times when people think poverty, they are ignorant and have contempt for the rich, and they have false humility.

We perish because of the lack of knowledge (Hosea 4:6). It is said if you want to hide something from poor people, put it in a book.

There is no excuse now for being ignorant. Access to information is readily available. Just about anything you want to know, learn or do can be ascertained on the internet. You are solely responsible for the development of your mind. Listen, knowledge brings about expansion and expansion brings about growth. If you want to do things that no one else has done, then you have to *"grow"* your mind. Never allow your mind to become idle.

Also, if you have disdain and contempt for rich people, then riches or rich people will never come your way. Psychologically, what you are doing is telling your brain to keep riches from you. We will never draw riches or wealth to us when we despise the rich. Here is something for you to think about. If they are rich and you are not, perhaps, *they know something that you do not know.* The financial knowledge that you do not know, is the financial knowledge that is being used against you.

Another erroneous thought in this area is false humility. The poorer we are, the closer we are to God. We are much more holy when we are broke. Some go as far to say that rich people cannot enter into the kingdom of God.

Wow...this is really crazy! I guess the devil's crowd is the only people who are supposed to have money. Not! The scripture tells us that the wealth of the wicked is laid up for the just. Who are the just? God's people! Also, Proverbs 15:6 says, "In the house of the righteous is much treasure...." If God does not want us to have wealth, then why put it in our house?

73

So where did this teaching develop? I tell you where -- from the story in the Bible about the rich young ruler? Like always, this has been misinterpreted. So let's look at this.

"And when he was gone forth into the way, there came one running and kneeled to him and asked him, Good Master, what shall I do that I may inherit eternal life?

And Jesus said unto him, why callest thou me good? There is none good but one, that is, God.

Thou knowest the commandments, do not commit adultery, do not kill, do not steal, do not bear false witness, defraud not, honour thy father and mother.

And he answered and said unto him, Master, all these have I observed from my youth.

Then Jesus beholding him loved him, and said unto him, one thing thou lackest: go thy way, sell whatsoever thou hast, and give to the poor, and thou salt have treasure in heaven: and come, take up the cross, and follow me.

And he was sad at that saying, and went away grieved: for he had great possessions.

And Jesus looked round about, and saith unto his disciples, How hardly shall they that have riches enter into the kingdom of God!

And the disciples were astonished at his words. But Jesus answereth again, and saith unto them, Children, how hard is it for them that trust in riches to enter into the kingdom of God.

It is easier for a camel to go through the eye of a needle, than for a rich man to enter into the kingdom of God.

Mark 10:17-25

Okay, let's examine some of these sentences line by line. First, *"Then Jesus beholding him loved him, and said unto him, one thing thou lackest: go thy way, sell whatsoever thou hast, and give to the poor, and thou shalt have treasure in heaven: and come, take up the cross, and follow me.*

This scripture is the granddaddy of them all. This is the Scripture people use to say God does not

76

want us rich or wealthy. They say it clearly says that God wants us to sell all of our worldly possessions and give to the poor. At face value, it might seem this way, but did it really say this?

The rich young ruler first came to Jesus seeking what he needed to do to get into heaven. Jesus told him about the Ten Commandments, and the ruler said, he had kept these since being a youth.

Then Jesus addressed the real problem – *"One thing thou lackest: go thy way, sell whatsoever thou hast, and give to the poor..."* – and the ruler left sad -- *"And he was sad at that saying, and went away grieved: for he had great possessions...how hard is it for them that **trust** in riches to enter into the kingdom of God."*

The ruler was more attached to his riches than he was attached to God. The real issue was his heart. He trusted in his riches more than he trusted in God.

Next, let's look at the statement, *"...go thy way, sell whatsoever thou hast, and give to the poor.* First, this statement did not say *give everything away*; it says *sell*. If God did not want the rich young ruler to have anything, He would have said give it away, but he said sell. Giving and selling have two different connotations. One you do not receive anything in exchange, and one you do.

Now, let's further clarify this, *"...give to the poor."* Notice this did not say, "...give *all* your money to the poor." It just says, give to the poor. I can give to the poor and still have money in my bank account. Again, the real motif to this story is that the rich young ruler trusted more in his riches than he did God. In actuality, this story complements the scripture in Timothy that says the love of money is the root of all evil. It gets back to the motive of why you want money. If you love money more than God, then money is your god. God is not mad with us because we have money, He just doesn't want money to have us.

Listen; there are lots of misguided people in this world. What you want to do is make up in your mind that you will not be one of them. We have been "hoodwinked" long enough. **And it is time we take the red cap back from the wolf.**

Poor People Have No Voice

One of the most powerful scriptures that echo that poverty is a curse is found in Ecclesiastes 9:16, *"Then said I, wisdom is better than strength: nevertheless the poor man's wisdom is despised, and his words are not heard."*

If you are broke and poor, you have "no" voice according to this scripture. You have no sphere of influence. Nobody wants to listen to you. This scripture says your words are not heard. You might be talking, but no one is listening to you. Why is this? You don't have any authority, no sphere of influence; you are broke! Who wants to listen to a broke person? I know I don't.

If I am already down, I need to talk to someone who can help bring me up and out of my situation. Poor people cannot do this.

Poor people cannot help other poor people get out of their situation. However, rich people can. The best way to help the poor is not be one of them. You cannot assist with anybody else's deliverance if you are where they are. A poor man has no voice, has no authority, and has no sphere of influence – "*...nevertheless the poor man's wisdom is despised, and his words are not heard,*" *(Ecclesiastes 9:16b).*

You have to dream big if you want to do great things for God. We must dream big enough for God to fit into your dreams. God is an infinite God and He does everything without measure – *"For he whom God hath sent speaketh the words of God: for God giveth not the Spirit by measure unto him"* (John 3:34). Author, Guy Peh says it this way, "The only limitations we have are the size of our dreams and the degree of our determination."

I encourage you to dream big and to dream the POSSIBLE dream.

Chapter 4

SEE BIG

(GOD HELPS US TO PASS THE TEST)

hat you see is what you get! Isn't it amazing how a simple statement like this has such a big implication? Our ability to see will always govern our ability to achieve. The power of vision is incredible. How we see or view things will affect our successes and failures, our ups and downs. Every choice we make will be connected to our visibility. We need to assess where we are to determine where we need to go. Vision plays an intricate part in this.

The Power of Vision

Vision is one of the main components to achieving all that God has for us. When we can clearly see (internally) how God wants to bless us; then our journey to achieving that success will be empowered. People without vision will be constantly ensnared in the mundane of life. And regret and disappointment will be the fruit of their journey.

Every person has a seed of greatness inside of them -- a seed that is waiting to grow and develop into all its potential within. Recorded in the book, *See Your Future, Be Your Book,* successful people look inward to the vision of their youth, and despite the chaos that may surround them, they continue to focus their sights on their dreams. They are the people who could see what they wanted in spite of their culture, environment or experience. They were not blinded by the clouds of the past, but led by the rays of the future." A compelling vision is conceived with purpose and clothed with passion.

The more clearly or profoundly that you can see the vision of God for your life, the more tenacious you will be in attaining it. This is why vision is so critical to your success. It empowers your journey and energizes your thoughts. A compelling vision will encourage and guide you along the way even though there are challenges.

Found in the book, *The Power of Passion,* are some attributes of vision:

- Vision doesn't just happen overnight – it is a process.
- Vision is easy to lose but hard to regain.
- Vision is absolutely necessary for survival.
- Visions must be written.
- Vision clarifies destination. Without it you are lost.
- Vision is God's way of getting you to think like Him – BIG
- Vision is within YOU – go find it.
- Vision never becomes a reality without action.
- True vision becomes a part of who you are.
- Where there is vision, there is provision.

People who have done great things for God have had great vision. They were people who could see farther than others. We cannot go any further than what we conceive in our mind. We can never change our location until we determine our destination. "Only he who can see the invisible can do the impossible," according to Frank Gaines.

When Abraham looked up into the sky and saw countless stars when God told him his descendants would be great, the stars became a focal point for his vision. No matter what his current situation was, he believed God, and it was counted unto him as righteousness (Romans 4:3).

Others may not see your vision; but it is more important that you see it. Where do you see yourself in five, ten or twenty? Do you see yourself owning a business? Do you see yourself as an entrepreneur? Or do you see yourself still working for somebody else? Whatever you see, you will be.

Dismantling the Grasshopper Complex

In Exodus when God delivered the Children of Israel out of the hand of Pharaoh, Moses, their great leader, was instructed to guide them to their promised land. As God was communing with Moses about their trip, God let Moses know that, yes, I have given you the land, but there are some people on the land who will have to be driven out *and* destroyed. There are some illegal squatters, but they will have to go. He reinforced His commitment to them, by letting them know that He was going to be with them all the way.

As the Israelites journey brought them closer to their promised land, Moses sent twelve spies into the land to survey it. Ten came back with an evil report and two (Joshua and Caleb) came back with a faith report. The ten that brought back the evil report were consumed by what they saw more in the natural than what was their prophetic destiny.

God had already told them, that He had given them the land. Their responsibility was to go in and possess it. If I give you a car, and you never come to pick it up, then you will never possess the car. Also, you will never reap the benefits of the car. Now, you might have to travel three hours to get it, but the car is still yours. Whether you have to ride by bus, plane or train, you can reap the benefit of the car when you take possession.

The problem here with the ten spies was that they did not want to go through the process to get what belonged to them. So many people are just like the ten spies. They want a college degree, but they don't want to spend two to four years in training to get the degree. Some might want a promotion on their job, but they have poor work ethics -- won't show up to work on time. What we invest our time in speaks volumes about our motivation and who we are.

There are no "freebies" in life, and what we have to realize is that we are swimming upstream anyway. So warfare is inevitable when trying to break out of old mindsets and detrimental environments.

There is a law of gravity that wants to keep you in the same place. The war is won if we believe we have won. Our minds are always the battleground for the fight.

The ten spies lost the battle in their minds. This is why they had a negative report. They let what they saw in the natural overtake them. They were more giant-conscious than God-conscious. Basically, the 10 spies had a grasshopper mentality.

One group said, "Did you see the size of those GIANTS?" The other team said, "Did you see the size of those GRAPES?" It is all about perception. Joshua and Caleb had the right perception.

Perspective and Purpose

Our God-given purpose is always tied to our ability to see what God sees. Controlling the thoughts that enter our minds is critical to our path of success. The uniqueness of our destiny requires a tamed mind, a mind that is not "running wild," but has been harnessed by the wisdom and counsel of God. To think that whatever just pops into our minds is true, is truly a fallacy.

One Christian leader once said, "I can't stop a bird from flying over my head, but I sure can stop him from making a nest in my hair!" This is what we have to do with wrong thinking and thoughts. We have to dismiss and annihilate them as soon as they are projected into our mind. And the ones that are already there, you have to dislodge them with truth by putting on the helmet of salvation.

In Ephesians, chapter six, Paul describes the six-piece armor of God. One of the pieces of the armor is the helmet of salvation. For the Roman soldiers the helmet was a very important piece of war garment. If someone hit or shot them in the head, they would be seriously injured, and to the point that they could no longer fight in a battle.

In addition, to the helmet, there was a visor as well. Protecting the eyes was another important element in battle. If soldiers could not see, it would impede possibly their victory. No matter what, their vision will be impaired.

We have to be properly clothed when in warfare with the devil and his allies. Know for a surety, the devil is a headhunter. If he can destroy our mind and warp our perspective, he can abort our future. We must protect our minds well because our eyes are the windows to our soul. "The light of the body is the eye: if therefore thine eye be single, thy whole body shall be full of light. But if thine eye be evil, thy whole body shall be full of darkness. If therefore the light that is in thee be darkness, how great is that darkness!" (Matthew 6:22-23).

Seeing Out of the Eyes of God

"Train your eyes to see evidence of his presence, not evidence of his absence," a quote by Wayne Cordeiro in his book, *Attitudes That Attracts Success.* The ability to see higher than our present state will require some type of divine intervention. To retrain the eyes to see what God sees is a process. When our eyes see things, they have the tendency to believe what they see based on the information that is always stored in the brain.

We are all predisposed to think and act a certain way. Not because we want to; it is just how we were cultivated (who, what, where). We have to train our eyes to see differently. We have to create a new reality. We have to train our eyes to see what God sees.

As the Prophet Elijah in the Old Testament came under attack one day by his enemy, he looked up and the enemy's horses and chariots had surrounded him. Immediately, his personal servant became fearful. Elijah comforted his servant and admonished him to fear not. Then he prayed that the Lord would open his eyes that he might see. He did and when he looked at the mountains, they were filled with horses and chariots of fire. They were completely surrounded by God's army (2 King 6:15-17).

The windows of our soul often get dirty and tainted through this journey called life. They become embedded with germs and soiled with all types of contaminations that are harmful to our future. So instead of our vision being clear, we see things through a glass darkly – *"For now we see through a glass, darkly..."* (I Corinthians 13:12). Therefore this threatens our baby (dream). This threatens our advancement. This threatens our increase.

The best way to ensure that we are seeing what God sees is to quickly reject everything that does not line up with the Word of God in our life. But here is the punch line: you have to know the Word of God. *"Let this mind be in you which was in Christ Jesus"* (Philippians 1:3). We can only attain the mind of Christ by staying and meditating on the Word of God. Let God's Word cleanse your perspective and develop you in the ways of life. Then, and only then, can you see what God sees.

To sum this chapter up, let me tell you about a story about two men who were in prison. And the story goes like this:

One night one of the prisoners, while lying in his bunk began sharing with the other prisoner the wonderful things he was seeing outside his window. He called to his cell mate in the bunk below, "Hey, wake up! Look at the stars! They are beautiful. Look!"

His cell mate said, "Aw, leave me alone."

"Come on, just look. The stars are brighter tonight than I have ever seen them."

Eventually, after much prodding, the cell mate turned over to look. After a brief glance, he growled, "I don't see any stars. All I see are bars."

This is how people in the world without a vision view things and how people with a vision view things. The Word of God says it this way, *"Where there is no vision, the people perish"* (Proverbs 29:18).

Chapter 5

ASK BIG
(GOD ANSWERS PRAYER REQUESTS)

Asking for what you want in the kingdom of God is one of the pediatric doctrines in the Word of God. Besides faith, asking is a pivotal aspect for us receiving our blessings from God and being financially solvent.

It is always amazing to me how many people just don't ask for what they want. Matthew 7:7-8 tells us that we must *first* ask in order to initially start the process of receiving in the kingdom of God. *"Ask, and it shall be given you; seek, and ye shall find; knock, and it shall be opened unto you. For every one that asketh receiveth; and he that seeketh findeth; and to him that knocketh it shall be opened."* Asking is always a part of the equation to our receiving all God has for us.

If you don't ask you will not have – "...ye have not, because ye ask not" (James 4:2). The thing about not asking is that you have **automatically** set yourself up for failure. You have a guaranteed "no" when you do not ask. So let's look at it this way. If you do not ask, you have a surety of a "no." But if you do ask, you have a fifty-fifty chance at least of getting a "yes." The mere fact that you will ask, strengthens your possibility of getting a favorable response. But let me let you in on a big secret. God said when you call on Him; He will answer you **and** show you great and mighty things (Jeremiah 33:3). So the odds are in your favor to receive what you ask for, you just have to ask. *"And this is the confidence that we have in him, that if we ask any thing according to his will, he heareth us: And if we know that he hears us, whatsoever we ask, we know that we have the petitions that we desired of him"* (James 5:14-15).

Whatever the devil says, think the opposite. He speaks with a "forked" tongue.

I am not completely sure why some people don't ask God for what they want, but I have been saved long enough that I have been able to identify some of the reasons. Here are a few of them:

1. They don't know what to ask for

The Bible says a double-minded person is unstable in all his ways. "But let him ask in faith, nothing wavering. *For he that wavereth is like a wave of the sea driven with the wind and tossed. For let not that man think that he shall receive any thing of the Lord. A double minded man is unstable in all his ways"* (James 1:6-8).

Being double-mindedness is being congruent with the nature of the devil. In the Bible, the devil is classified as a "serpent." A serpent has a forked tongue, which is synonymous with duplicity. Duplicity speaks of double-minded of speech, action, thought, and deceit. Never trust anything the devil tells you.

If he says you are not going to make it, know that you can make it. If he says you will never amount to anything, know that you will be somebody. If he tells you, you will never get married, say, "Praise God, I know my mate is on the way." Whatever the devil says, think the opposite. He speaks with a "forked" tongue.

As a believer, you can't afford to "go out this way." You have to become single-minded. You have to gird up the loins of your mind (I Peter 1:13). Do whatever it takes to get rid of double-mindedness. Yes, I know one of the reasons some people struggle with wavering is that they don't have any peace or joy in their lives. But the Bible says let not your heart be troubled for in this world you will have trials and tribulations. It also tells us to be anxious for nothing, but in everything with prayer and thanksgivings we are to make our requests known unto Him. Listen; warfare is inevitable. But what we do with and in warfare determines our outcome.

2. They don't have a winner's attitude

Our attitude has a lot to do with how we perceive things in life. Also, it has a lot to do with our faith. The language of faith is being thankful and kind. Faith encourages us to persevere even when we want to "throw in the towel." If we *know* that God will deliver us out of a situation even though we do not *see* the manifestation, then we can praise and thank Him in faith —*"That ye be not slothful, but followers of them who through faith and patience inherit the promises...For when God made a promise to Abraham, because he could swear by no greater, he sware by himself...And so, after he had patiently endured, he obtained the promise"* (Hebrews 6:12-15).

Having a negative attitude is of the devil. God is about peace, love, joy, and righteousness. He is about showering His people with His glory and goodness. It is the devil that makes us think otherwise. God is about blessing, not cursing. God is about giving, not taking. God is about sharing, not hoarding. God is about love, not hate. God is about freedom, not captivity. He is certainly not about you being broke, busted and disgusted. He is about you having life and having it more abundantly. *"If ye then, being evil, know how to give good gifts unto your children: how much more shall your heavenly Father give the Holy Spirit to them that **ask** him?"* (Luke 11:13).

We have to ask God for what we want. It is all right to ask God for things — *"Be careful for nothing; but in every thing by prayer and supplication with thanksgiving **let your***

requests be made known unto God"
(Philippians 4:6).   However, I found out if we
would just seek God more – "Seek ye first the
kingdom of God and his righteousness" – some
of the things we want will automatically come
to pass – *"and all of these things shall be
added unto you"* (Matthew 6:33).

We have to develop and operate out of a
winning attitude at all times. We have to
manage our continuity in this area.   In the
universe, we attract what we are. So if we are
releasing negative energy into the world, then
negative energy we will receive back. But if we
release positive energy into the world, then
positive energy we will receive back.   It is
about sowing and reaping...sowing and
reaping...sowing and reaping – what you sow,
you will reap.

We, in the body of Christ, have to learn how to
function out of a mentality that generates

success for us. And having a negative attitude certainly will not cultivate the desired success that many of us want in life. For some, I know it is environment, but for most, it's just limited thinking. We allow the world to dictate to us what we can or cannot do, or what we can be or cannot be.

Our mirror or gauge is never the world's systems. Our mirror is the Word of God. *"But whoso looketh into the perfect law of liberty, and continueth therein, he being not a forgetful hearer, but a doer of the word, this man shall be blessed in his deed"* (James 1:25). When we do it God's way, we will be blessed.

Keeping our minds on track is an ongoing process. This is why we have to be in a lifelong personal development program. We should be like wine – getting better as we age. Each of us has been placed in the middle of a world filled with worldly perspectives and philosophies. But here's the wonder of God's design: Although we live in the midst of a "crooked and perverse generation" (Philippians 2:15), none of that crooked perverseness is supposed to get inside of us! Your attitude will either protect you or defeat you in the midst of storms.

When we deal with negative things, we have to always see these negative circumstances changing. When we encounter problems, we are to speak of these problems as always changing. For instance, If someone says, "You have a problem." Your response should be, "Yes, but it's changing!" If someone says, "You have financial problems." You should say, "Yes, but it's changing!" If someone says, "You are not doing so well." You say, "Yes, but it's changing!" If someone says, "You have a bad marriage!" Your response should be, "Yes, but it's changing!"

Do you see and understand the pattern here? When you speak that the situation is changing, hope comes alive. Then your dark situation attracts light. We all need to do an attitude check.

Once there was a story of a man who went to the doctor because he was experiencing pain all over his body. The man complained to the doctor that wherever he touches his body, it hurts. He wanted to know if he were just getting old or senile. If he touches his knee, it hurts. If he touches his arm, it hurts. If he touches his stomach, it hurts. The doctor did a full body x-ray. The man said, "Doc, did you find the problem." Stroking his chin, the doctor slowly began, "I think I have found the reason why everything you touch hurts." "Well, tell me!" the man anxiously said. The doctor pointed to the x-ray, "Your body is fine, your finger is broken."

Our attitude is like that finger. If our attitude stinks, everything around us will reflect this attitude. If our attitude is great, everything around us will reflect this greatness.

How is your attitude? If it is not where it needs to be, then start today to see things more positively. If you do this often enough, you will develop a winning attitude.

3. They don't know who they are in Christ Jesus

We are born with an innate proclivity to rule, reign and win. Anything inside us that tells us differently is of the devil. Having a slavery mentality is unnatural. A correct functionality of a Christian's brain constantly secretes thoughts of being a predator, not a prey. We are built to dominate and manage the works of God's hands (Genesis 1:26). We co-exist in high places with the Father and Son. We were born to be and sit in "High Places." *"And hath raised us up together, and made us sit together in heavenly places in Christ Jesus...For we are his workmanship, created in Christ Jesus unto good works, which God hath before ordained that we should walk in them"* (Ephesians 2:6-10).

We can be up in a down world because of Ephesians 2:6 -- *"And hath raised us **UP** together, and made us **sit together in HEAVENLY places** in Christ Jesus...."* We were born to taste the grapes. God has made us to sit with Him. If you are still struggling about who you are in Christ Jesus, I submit to you that you are struggling because you have the wrong concept of God. We can teach you all day about how you are seated in heavenly places with God. But if your concept of God is that He is a "deadbeat dad," and that His kingdom is full of dilapidated buildings, and that the only thing He is interested in is self-glorification, then your concept is warped.

You will see being seated with God as a debated position instead of an elevated position.

When you are born again, you are a part of a new family of God. You become an heir with the Father and a joint-heir with the Son (Romans 8:17). You are no longer a beggar and a stranger meandering along in life, but you are a king and a priest unto your God (Ephesians 2:19, Revelation 1:5-6). And you are not just any kind of priest, but you are a part of a royal lineage. *"But ye are a chosen generation, a royal priesthood, an holy nation, a peculiar people; that ye should shew forth the praises of him who hath called you out of darkness into his marvelous light"* (I Peter 2:9).

Many people know who God is. Some people know who the devil is, but most people don't know who they are in Christ.

Now, God sees you as being valuable – worthy to carry His glorious Word. *"But we have this treasure in earthen vessels, that the excellency of the power may be of God, and not of us"* (II Corinthians 4:7). You are treasure in God's eyes. As well, you are the apple of God's eye. What you have to do now is embrace your new reality and identity.

"⁹For the Lord's portion is his people; Jacob is the lot of his inheritance.

¹⁰He found him in a desert land, and in the waste howling wilderness; he led about, he instructed him, he kept him as the apple of his eye.

¹¹As an eagle stirreth up her nest, fluttereth over her young, spreadeth abroad her wings, taketh them, beareth them on her wings:

¹²So the Lord alone did lead him, and there was no strange god with him.

¹³He made him ride on the HIGH places of the earth, that he might eat the INCREASE of the fields; and he made him to suck honey out of the rock, and oil out of the flinty rock.

¹⁴Butter of kine, and milk of sheep, with fate of lambs, and rams of the breed of Bashan, and goats, with the fat of kidneys of wheat; and thou didst drink the pure blood of the grape" (Deuteronomy 32:9-14).

The **HIGH** place in God is a place of increase. It is a place that exults the majesty of God and the riches of His glory. "HIGH-minded" Christians will always eat the pure "blood" of the grapes. While some Christians might be eating from the trough of the pig, others are eating from the table of the king. It is all how you see yourself in Christ. Many people know who God is. Some people know who the devil is, but most people don't know who they are in Christ.

If you want increase and to experience miracles in your life, then knowing who you are in Christ is a must. You cannot find until you define. You cannot ask for something if you do not know what you need. Jesus said to blind Bartimaeus in Mark's gospel, *"What wilt thou that I should do unto thee?"* The blind man knew exactly what he wanted -- *"The blind man said unto him, Lord, that I might receive my sight"* (Mark 10:51). You cannot be a successful Christian if you don't know who you are in Christ.

4. They are afraid of change

Change is inevitable. Many of the inventions and medical breakthroughs were brought about because of change. Change is the cost for progress. Many of the things we deem sacred today were invented because of change. However, when some of these changes were presented at its embryonic stage, they were rejected. Change has always been a challenge for man.

As more and more studies have been done on "change," what researchers have found is that change was not the problem, but "transition" was. According to these researchers, most changes happen instantaneously – loss of job, death of spouse, loss to income, etc. Therefore, it is not "change" that challenges most people, but rather it is the transition. Now that this has happened, how do I transition into this new reality? And who am I now?

This stage is what researchers call the neutral zone. In the book, *The Way of Transition*, the author declares that there are three dimensions to change – **Ending, Neutral Zone and Beginning.** He talks about situational changes – loss of job, new baby, etc., and transition, which by definition is the process of letting go of the way things used to be and then taking hold of the way they subsequently become.

Change is to make different, but transition is the passage way. So what most people resist is transition. In transition, things seems chaotic. What's happening is that now people have to explore and discover their new reality. The author also identified three tenets that are a part of these three   primary states:

- Disenchantment -- Transition makes a person feel that not only is a piece of his or her reality gone, but that everything that had seemed to be reality was simply an enchantment.

- Disidentification -- Transition does not simply disenchant; it breaks up your old identity too.

- Disorientation – Feeling lost, don't know which end is up.

While transition brings on all of these feelings and anxieties, the truth of the matter, though, "transition" is really how we come to terms with change. We must ask ourselves, when in transition, "What is it that I need to let go? What is it that I need to learn and unlearn?" There is a saying, "The chief object of education is not to learn things but to unlearn things."

Now that you know the difference between change and transition, let's look at change in relation to our text – Some people don't ask because they are afraid of changing.

The kingdom of God is a kingdom in motion. It is an active vibrant kingdom. Within its DNA are energizing forces of transformation and reformation.

"Knowing this, that our old man is crucified with him, that the body of sin might be destroyed, that henceforth we should not serve sin" (Romans 6:6).

"And be not conformed to this world: but be ye transformed by the renewing of your mind..." (Romans 12:2)

"Who hath delivered us from the power of darkness, and hath translated us into the kingdom of his dear Son" (Colossians 1:13)

"The word of God is quick, and powerful, and sharper than any twoedged sword, piercing even to the dividing asunder of soul and spirit, and of the joints and marrow, and is a

discerner of the thoughts and intents of the heart." (Hebrew4:12)

"I am the true vine, and my Father is the husbandman. Every branch in me that beareth not fruit he taketh away: and every branch that beareth fruit, he purgeth it, that it may bring forth more fruit." (John 15:1-2)

When God wants us to change, it is always about our welfare. It is about Him releasing His goodness toward us. Regardless, whether He is correcting or caressing us, it is about our success. It is about our destiny. So don't be afraid to ask for what you want from God. Yes, you don't always know everything about a situation, but your refusal to change will not guarantee that whatever you care about will stay the same.

When we refuse to change, and resist God's leading, life can become even more miserable. Henceforth, the pain of staying the same becomes greater than the pain of changing. In fact, in order to achieve continuity of what we do know or have, being willing to change is the only way to protect that which already exists.

The definition of insanity is doing the same thing repeatedly and expecting a different result. If you are not satisfied with where you are in life now, then resolve the fact that you will have to change. Settle the issue in your heart.

Many people want to do great things for God, but they don't want to do the things that produce greatness in their lives. Every dream is going to cost you something. When God looks for someone to release His greatness through; He looks for those who are faithful and busy. He does not look for lazy and manipulative servants. *"Therefore be ye also ready: for in such an hour as ye think not the Son of man cometh. Who then is a faithful and wise servant, whom his lord hath made ruler over his household, to give them meat in due season? Blessed is that servant, whom his lord, when he cometh shall find so <u>doing</u>. Verily I say unto you, that he shall make him ruler over all his goods"* (Matthew 24:44- 47).

Many people make New Year's resolutions every year to change. But statistically, only 55 percent of the people in America who make a resolution keep it for one month; 40 percent keep it for six months; and only 19 percent keep it for two years. Looking at this rate of success lets us know that most people are not committed to change.

If God is going to use us in this hour and/or make us a steward over much, He needs to know that we are pliable and flexible. Are you willing to bend when He tells you to bend? Again, change is inevitable, so go ahead and prepare yourself for greatness. And ask God for what you want.

Preparation in the Greek denotes equipment, readiness. When you prepare for God's glory in your life, you will have everything you need to be successful in life. You would be fully equipped. God wants you blessed. He wants you to do great things for Him. So don't be afraid of change.

The Weight of Glory

With every realm of glory and promotion in your life will come a greater measure of responsibility to manage and steward. This is why you have to prepare for the greatness of God in your life. When you ask for big things, you just might get them. Every increase attracts an increase of warfare. This is not for you to be afraid of, but for you to know this is all part of the equation. *"For our light affliction, which is but for a moment, worketh for us a far more exceeding and eternal weight of glory"* (II Corinthians 4:17).

Many of you have heard how people have won the lottery and some had played for over 20 years, waiting for that big moment. Well, that big moment came, but they were not prepared for it. Their knowledge base or mental capacity could not handle the influx of the amount of income they had won. What happened? Most of these people ended up broke within a year.

Your personal growth and development must measure up to your financial development. If not, you will not be able to maintain and hold onto this type of wealth. There is nothing wrong with asking God for wealth, just prepare your mind. Do your homework. Read books about finances, budgeting and investments. The more prepared you are before you receive the blessings of God, the more equipped you will be to handle the things of God.

Ask and you will receive (Mark 11:23-24). Expect God to do great things through you. Hannah asked God for a child and she conceived a child. *"And she vowed a vow, and said, O Lord of hosts, if thou wilt indeed look on the affliction of thine handmaid, and remember me, and not forget thine handmaid, but wilt give unto thine handmaid a man child, then I will give him unto the Lord all the days of his life, and there shall no razor come upon his head...Wherefore it came to pass, when the time was come about after Hannah had conceived, that she bare a son, and called his name Samuel saying, because I have **asked** him of the Lord"* (I Samuel 1:11-12).

There is an old Chinese proverb that goes something like this, "If you expect nothing, you will not be disappointed."

Chapter 6

PRAY BIG

(GOD GIVES POWER IN PRAYER)

There is power in prayer. Power is given to men who pray! God's people will always receive what God has for them when they are a people of prayer. The role that prayer plays in the developmental process of the realization of dreams and visions is incredible. If you want your dreams and visions realized in an exponential way, then build a strong prayer life. Prayer will eliminate and eradicate much of the debris you pick up in life as you exist on this earth.

Prayer like words is a resource tool. It is a tool that is tied to the infinite and tangible. It is a spiritual element that energizes and creates into existence things that are not as though they are. Therefore, empowered by the Spirit of God, we can pray BIG!

Our Father Abraham is a good example of praying big. He prayed big and he got big. He called things that were not as though they were. *"Therefore it is of faith, that it might be by grace; to the end the promise might be sure to all the seed; not to that only which is of the law, but to that also which is of the faith of Abraham; who is the father of us all. (As it is written, I have made thee a Father of many nations,) before him whom he believed, even God, who quickeneth the dead, and calleth those things which be not as though they were. Who against hope believed in hope, that he might become the father of many nations, according to that which was spoken, So shall thy seed be"* (Romans 4:16-18).

The Bible says the just shall live by faith. I am thankful for this statement, so I don't have to wonder any more (nor you), why I am not receiving something that I should be receiving. Why I am not where I want to be and why I am not getting what I want to have.

It's not God's fault, it's my fault. I am the one who is supposed to be living by faith.

Whatever we have now, our faith has done the work. If you don't like what you have, work on your faith. God said He will reward those who diligently seek Him. A reward is something good, not bad. If bad things are happening to you all the time, you need to check yourself and see whom you are seeking. Are you seeking God or are you seeking things?

We have to activate the Word in prayer to receive God's blessings. We have to stand in faith and believe whether we see a manifestation or not. The God kind of faith is the faith that speaks and believes and believes and speaks -- *"Whosoever says to this mountain be thou removed... and does not doubt in his heart"* (Mark 11:23).

Often we spend time in prayer telling God how big our problems are, but we need to tell our problems how big our God is. Whatever mountains that are standing in our way, we need to speak to them. Our mountains need to hear our voice. "Have faith in God" means have the God kind of faith.

The more you yield to the lordship of Jesus, the more you will increase the manifestation and the flow of the kingdom of God in your lives.

Creating An Atmosphere For Change

When we pray, we invoke God's presence in our midst, which creates an atmosphere for change. Prayer is "speaking" or "muttering" words to God. It is utilizing words to invite God to move on our behalf and for others. One evangelist said, "We can't say until we pray." This is a powerful little statement.

This statement challenges us to align our words up with only the things that come from the throne of God -- *"Thy kingdom come, thy will be done."* If only we would do this. If we would just speak the words God tells us to speak in prayer we will be successful in prayer.

II Chronicles 7:14, lets us know that we are the agent of change. When we pray big (correctly, completely aligned with the Word of God), then the heaven will open for us. *"If my people, which are called by my name, shall humble themselves, and pray, and seek my face, and turn from their wicked ways; then will I hear from heaven, and will forgive their sin, and will heal their land."* **The heavens will open when we pray big!**

God is A Big God

God is not afraid of our prayer requests. I believe sometimes, people pray mediocre prayers or they are scared to ask God for things because they don't think He wants to do anything for them. Get over yourself and stop bringing God down to your level. The more you yield to the lordship of Jesus, the more you will increase the manifestation and the flow of the kingdom of God in your lives.

Our prayers must be filled with faith and energized by our passion. If we want to do big things for God, then we have to make sure that we pray big.

The book of I Chronicles, chapter 4:10, *Jabez prayed a big prayer. It says, "And Jabez called on the God of Israel, saying, oh that thou wouldest bless me indeed, and enlarge my coast, and thine hand might be with me, and that thou wouldest keep me from evil, that it may not grieve me! And God granted him that which he requested."*

It says God granted what he requested. What if Jabez had prayed some mediocre prayer? The inference here is that he would have gotten what he requested. Instead, he asked God to bless him and to enlarge his territory. Expand me God, expand my sphere of influence, expand my mind was in essence what Jabez was seeking -- I want to do greater things for you. But the secret to Jabez's answered prayer was not just his prayer, but his heart. He asked God to keep him from evil and to always be ever-present in his life – "...*And thine hand might be with me, and that* thou wouldest keep me from evil, that it may not grieve me!"

The crux of this prayer request is in this statement – a humble heart. A heart that is not humble or pure before God is a heart that is heartened and rebellious. It is a heart filled with pride and hidden agendas. This is why God requires believers to humble themselves first before He hears their prayers – *"If my people, which are called by my name, shall humble themselves, and pray."*

Keys to Receiving Your Miracle book says, "Humility is not denying the power you have. It is realizing that the power comes through you, not from you."

We must humble ourselves so God can effectively use us in the kingdom of God.

Building Character Through Prayer

Prayer has a way of subduing. This is why it is hard for prideful people to pray. It is best we humble ourselves versus God humbling us. Regardless, prayer is a wonderful catalyst in assisting in building character in people. It is hard to fight with one another, when we are praying. The deeper your character, the easier it is for you to develop an attitude or mindset for change.

What happens in prayer is that it softens hearts. It turns stony hearts into hearts of flesh. Often in prayer, people cry. What is happening? Their hearts are being tenderized. God is turning their stony and hard hearts into flesh. This is why we need to have more God-centered prayer meetings in our churches. It just might eliminate some of our problems.

Chapter 7

BE BIG

GOD CREATES THE REAL McCOY

The secret to our continuing success in God today is learning how to master "being." Because so much of what we do in Christ is preparing us for our "next," we have to learn how to "BE" in our present state. The book, *Secrets of the Millionaire Mind,* says the order of success is BE, DO and HAVE. To be paid the best, we must be the best.

Being big is more than just mere words. It is about understanding your universal role in life and providing the universe with whatever is needed to deliver it to you. Of course, the secret here is knowing what you are called to do in this earth. It is about working out your own soul salvation. It is about fulfilling the kingdom's mandate upon your life. After all, is not this what we are after -- to fulfill God's promise for our lives?

It is becoming the "REAL MCCOY." It is living the abundant life that God ordained for all of His children.

Living in the Now

We live our lives looking forward, and we understand our lives looking backward, but we frame our tomorrows by our actions today – *"This is the day that the Lord has made."*

Your miracle is in the moment. Your life is made up of connecting dots that miracles ride upon. It is a sequential succession of miracle encounters. Your miracle is moments in the "now" that will never be repeated.

As believers, we must live in the now. We must look for the now miracles in God. Successful people move in the now. *Now* faith is the substance of all things hoped for... (Hebrews 11:1).

Know Your Worth

I shared a lot about personal worth in an earlier chapter, but I want to elaborate on a few more things regarding to what you offer from a service and product standpoint.

Some of you devalue the services and products you offer in your business by charging too little. There have been people who have chosen to work with someone who charged more for a service or product because the one that had the lower price caused them to be skeptical of the value.

Sometimes we as Christians look at business wrong. We try to help everybody out in the church by giving them a deal and a discount. Let me help you out here. You will go broke doing this. Now, let me clear up some things.

First, you are in business. A business is established to produce a profit. Question: Are you a business or a charitable organization? You need to decide today. If you conclude you are a business, then do a market analysis on your service or product prices, and base your prices on your survey. If you want to charge less, this is okay, just make sure it is comparable to the market. Know this; you will be paid in direct proportion to the value you deliver according to the marketplace.

Now, if you realize in your heart that you want to be a charitable organization instead of a business, this is okay. Ask for donations and gifts for your service. Therefore, you will not devalue your product or service by charging so little for them?

Living in the NOW is knowing your worth!

Develop Your Gifts and Talents

There is so much information readily available on the internet now that everyone can be proficient in just about any subject matter. And many of the tutorial programs are free.

If you are applying for a job and you lack knowledge or skills in a certain area, do some research and strengthen yourself in this area. You can only be as big as your thinking. What you want to do is become an expert in your area. By continuing to learn and grow in your craft, you will **"BE."** Millionaire Myron Golden says in his book, *From Trash Man to Cash Man,* "Rich people educate themselves, poor people entertain themselves." Which one are you?

You have to learn how to raise the bar for your own self. If you are proficient in French, learn how to speak Spanish. In Christ, we need to be looking always for ways to improve ourselves. Let's not become stale bread. Let's "be" today's man or today's woman. There is nothing wrong with being the best. We are told in the Word of God that we are to make our callings and elections sure. *"Wherefore the rather, brethren, give diligence to make your calling and election sure: for if ye do these things, ye shall never fall"* (II Peter 1:10). This is what we need to be doing every day of our lives. Every day is an opportunity for us to improve ourselves. *"A wise man will hear, and will increase learning; and a man of understanding shall attain unto wise counsels"* (Proverbs 1:5).

You show people your value by how much time you waste.

We have been hand crafted by God and endowed with at least one specific quality or gift to be a blessing to the world. And it is our responsibility to develop that gift to its full potential. Even though we have been called to taste the grapes, they are not placed in our mouths, but in our reach. There is a genius inside of all of us screaming to come out. So release your genius!

Manage Your Time

Millionaires and billionaires are always conscious of time. Only fools waste time. We have to learn how to manage time, if we want to operate in the land that flows with "milk and honey."

Time is so precious and it is lost every second of the day. Never take time for granted. It is not something you can replenish. Once it is gone, it is gone.

You show people your value by how much time you waste. Myron Golden also said in his book, *From Trash Man to Cash Man,* that if you are not making $25,000 a month, you need to throw your television away. A television is an income reducing entity.

A television causes people to be consumers and not producers. From this point on after reading this book, please assess your time and your spending habits. If what you buy is not a wealth producing tool, then leave it in the store. It is said that if you look at what a person spends his or her money on, it will identify that person's habits and passions. Some might be good; some might be bad. Eliminate the bad today and start BEcoming a producer today.

People make billions of dollars off you being a consumer -- wasting your money on things that ultimately do not add value to your net worth. Get smart and make your own millions. Mark Victor Hansen, a multimillionaire and *Chicken Soup for the*

Soul author, said that you making your million would not take anything from someone else. He went on to say in his book, *One Minute Millionaire,* that there are over 28 trillion dollars in our economy, so don't worry about this at all. We all can get our million, and have plenty left over.

Manage your time well. Time wasters are not kingdom-minded people. People who sit around joking and talking about nothing all the time have designed a model of failure for their life – *"Go to the ant slugge,"* -- it is time we break those negative counterproductive behaviors and BE today who you want to BE in the future.

Write the Vision

If you write something down, it increases the chances of it coming to pass significantly. This is a wonderful principle of habit-forming. Not only does it challenge you to inventory your souls, but it also gives you a written structured document to meditate over and birth into existence.

Habakkuk says, "Write the vision, make it plain and it will surely come to pass" (Chapter 2:2-3). Luke tells us in chapter 14:28-31, *"For which of you, intending to build a tower, sitteth not down first, and counteth the cost, whether he have sufficient to finish it.?...Or what king, going to make war against another king, sitteth not down first, and consulteth whether he be able with ten thousand to meet him that cometh against him with twenty thousand."*

Writing something out is a point of sealing. From the educational system to the governmental system to the medical arena, and especially the legal system, having a written document is a part of establishing truth. This is why we are all encouraged to prepare a will. Because when we die, our will outlines our wishes as to how we want our personal property and estates dispersed. And if we have young children, it will also share who we want to have guardianship over them and how to handle any other financial matters for them. So having a written document is very important for our wishes and desires to be followed.

In addition, in biblical times, God often admonished His leaders in the Old Testament to prepare written documents as a memorial, testimony and covenant for the children of Israel. As well, kings' decrees had to be written in order for a law to be established. Here are some Scriptures for confirmation.

*"And the Lord said unto Moses, **write this for a memorial in a book,** and rehearse it in the ears of Joshua: for I will utterly put out the remembrance of Amalek from under heaven"* (Exodus 17:14).

*"And the Lord said unto Moses, **write thou these words**: for after the tenor of these words I have made a covenant with thee and with Israel"* Exodus 34:27

"And the Lord spake unto Moses, saying, Speak unto the children of Israel, and take of every one of them a rod according to the house of

136

their fathers, of all their princes according to the house of their fathers twelve rods: **write thou every man's name upon his rod.** *And thou shalt write Aaron's name upon the rod of Levi: for one rod shall be for the head of the house of their fathers. And thou shalt lay them up in the tabernacle of the congregation before the testimony, where I will meet with you"* (Numbers 17:1-4).

"And thou shalt write them upon the posts of thy house, and on thy gates. *And it shall be, when the Lord thy God shall have brought thee into the land which he sware unto thy fathers, to Abraham, to Isaac, and to Jacob, to give thee great and goodly cities, which thou buildest not,"* (Deuteronomy 6:9-10).

"And because of all this we make a sure covenant, **and write it;** *and our princes, Levites, and priests, seal unto it,"* (Nehemiah 9:38).

*"**Write ye also for the Jews,** as it liketh you, in the king's name, and seal it with the King's ring: **for the writing which is written in the king's name, and sealed with the king's ring, may no man reverse.**"* (Esther 8:8).

So having a written document stating your wishes and desires is an old and common practice in biblical times. But the key that I want you to get out of all of this, is that it was the "writing down" of these desires that established it.

Do not take this part of the process lightly. Writing your goals and visions down is a *major* component to your success model. It helps seal it. It helps establish it. And it is an energizing force that propels it into existence. If you have not written down your dreams and visions yet, let me encourage you today to prepare a vision statement document today. Don't wait, don't put it off, do it today.

Align yourself With Like-Minded People

Out of all the things I have shared thus far, this is a big one. If you are going to move up, go up, think big and be big in society, you have to align yourself with like-minded people. Your associations do define you. The Bible says that evil communication corrupts good manners (I Corinthians 15:33). Here are some different translations of this verse:

- "Do not be misled. Bad associations corrupt good morals." (Modern Language).

- "Don't be fooled by those who say such things. If you listen to them you will start acting like them" (Living Bible).

- "Do not be deceived: bad company ruins good morals" (Revised Standard).

- "Do not be misled: bad company corrupts good character." (New International Version).

It does matter who your associates are. If you are believing God to come out of poverty, then you need to be talking with people who are living an abundant life. If you want to be successful in business, then you need to be hanging out with successful business people. If you want to have a happy marriage, then you need to be spending time with couples who have a happy marriage. It is not the other way around. You have to really fight against the familiarity spirit that breeds contempt. It will keep you in a cycle of poverty and defeat if you don't fight against it relentlessly.

You see, because we are designed to be connectors or for connection, we have a built in magnet that draws us to people like us. So we have to engage and enlarge our minds by putting new information into it, so that the law of attraction will draw into our lives people who are from different backgrounds than those we are accustomed to.

What will this do? This will open up your life to experience another level of influence that probably you have never experienced. We really are not as independent as we think we are. Rather, we are interdependent. Our lives are all intertwined together.

As we move up, everything about our lives must change and expand. It is what I said earlier, exposure brings about expansion and expansion brings about change. Five or ten years from now, you should not be the "same" person. You should be constantly growing and developing in your craft – gifts and callings in God. If not, you have developmental problems.

It is like a child in its developmental stage. If a child is five years old and ten years later the child looks the same – has not grown at all, then doctors would classify this child as having developmental problems. Then the doctors would do an examination on the child and run all kinds of tests to see what is wrong.

Sometimes the child might have genetic issues. Sometimes the child might have bone problems. Other times the child might have mental challenges. But sometimes the child might have been malnourished. Regardless of the outcome, a systematic plan will be designed to correct the situation.

Some Christians are growth stunted. They have developmental problems. They come to the "table" with all kinds of issues or they were so "damaged" in life that they cannot see beyond their pain. And the devil has them tied up in their minds and emotions. But the good news is they do not have to stay this way.

God is always challenging us to live in the NOW and not in the past. We should not be a prisoner to our past. If we cannot get beyond our past, then reach out for help. Help is at reach.

Everybody needs an advisor, a mentor (coach), and a sponsor in his or her life. Proverbs 13:20 says, *"He that walketh with wise men shall be wise: but a companion of fools shall be destroyed."* Proverbs 15:22 also says, *"Without counsel purposes are disappointed: but in the multitude of counselors they are established."*

Carla A. Harris, a Wall Street veteran who wrote the book, *Expect To Win* defines an advisor as someone who can answer your discrete career questions, but not necessarily in context of your broader career goal.

But a mentor is someone who does all of the above, but gives you more specific tailored career advice. You can share with them the good, the bad and the ugly. On the other hand, a sponsor is someone who uses his or her influence to move you up in your career or bring you to the "table."

The more diverse these people are the greater the breadth and depth of advice and knowledge you will gain from them. How much you grow and how fast you grow depends on your knowledge and your associations. According to Guy Peh, international missionary and evangelist, "Association brings manifestation. The right association will bring the right manifestation. The wrong association will bring the wrong manifestation."

The secret to Esther's queen promotion was her relationship with Mordecai. The secret to Elisha's double-portion anointing was his association with Elijah. The secret to Joshua' great leadership was his commitment to Moses. The secret to Samuel's keen spiritual discernment was his association with Eli. The secret of Timothy's spiritual growth was his relationship with Paul. The secret to the twelve disciples powerful preaching was their association with Jesus.

Being with the right people does matter. Today, you need to make up in your mind what type of person you are going to "BE." It is said there are three types of people:

- People who make things happen.
- People who watch things happen.
- People who wonder what happened.

Which one are you going to "BE?"

We were made to rule and reign!

Ephesians, Chapters 1- 2:

He has blessed us (1:3).

He has chosen us (1:4).

He has predestined us (1:5).

He has accepted us (1:6).

He has redeemed us (1:6).

He has forgiven us (1:7).

He has abounded toward us in wisdom (1:8).

He has made known to us the mystery of his will (1:9).

He has sealed us (1:13).

He has enlightened our understanding (1:18).

He has raised us to sit in Heavenly places (2:6).

BE BIG...BECAUSE YOUR HEAVENLY FATHER IS BIG – *"The earth is the Lord's and the fullness thereof; the world, and they that dwell therein"* (Psalm 24:1)

BE BIG...BECAUSE YOUR HEAVENLY FATHER THINKS BIG – *"Now unto him that is able to do exceeding abundantly above all that we ask or think, according to the power that worketh in us"* (Ephesians 3:20).

Someone once wrote that life is a seminar. We were enrolled in it at birth. We can't get out of it. We came into this seminar with no instructional manual. So you owe it to yourself to enjoy life and be a winner.

Expect the best in life -- the absolute best. Learn to live in the **NOW!** Determine in your mind, you deserve the best. When you expect more, you get more.

Bottom line: YOU CAN HAVE WHAT YOU SAY IF YOU STOP SAYING WHAT YOU HAVE!!!